ROOK

To a rook called Barnacle Fred

ROOK

DEBORAH KING

Hamish Hamilton
London

FEBRUARY is the cruellest month. The rooks are restless, flying home in straggling flocks to roost in the tallest trees, rivals in their struggle to survive. They are tired and hungry and anxious for the first signs of a new spring.

It is a dead and dying time. There is no warmth from the sun to encourage new growth. The cold North winds bring rain and snow, while overnight frosts freeze the soil to stone. The land has lost its colours and lies asleep, waiting for the sun to crack the ice and bring new life.

The sun, rarely seen, turns red behind the hills of Rockfield. And as the moon appears, rooks from far and wide, tumble, twist and dive into the darkening sky and fly until night falls – their reckless calls the only sound to break the wintry silence.

A NEW DAY breaks and young Rook looks around. The land is very still and the sky is changing. The gathering thunder clouds cast a dull, disturbing light across the valley and only new-born lambs give voice to their fear, their plaintive cries echoing on the distant hillsides.

Rook sits on Little Ancre Hill and waits while older rooks take up frantic flight with jackdaws. Unsettled by the atmosphere he joins them. The farmer watches, guided by their better instincts. Their aerial acrobatics warn him of the winter weather still to come, and heeding their warning, he moves his sheep to sheltered ground.

March is full of surprises. The scattered snowdrops and the few spring daffodils will not survive another snowdrift and the recent bursts of sunlight have brought some ewes to lamb too early. For far beyond Deepholm where the birds are flying, Buckholt Wood stands in the shadow of a storm. And high on the distant hill, the clouds now thick with snow start rolling around the pines of Pyefinch Wood.

WINTER returns to Rockfield. A thick carpet of snow covers all but the bare trees and hedges, the only shelter for small birds and mammals suffering from this cruel weather. The fields look clean and tidy with this sudden change – a strange perfection, hiding many problems.

The rooks fly rings around their roosts, loudly voicing their protest. They cannot forage and resort to scavenging around the village. Some give up the fight and die of cold during the long night while herons, wild duck and geese repeatedly trace the margins and inlets of the River Monnow in search of a break in the ice. Only the hedgehogs and dormice have found the answer and sleep soundly through these treacherous months.

The farmer tends his scattered sheep and counts his losses. Rook's relatives, the magpies, crowd together in spirited defiance of the cold. The rest of Rockfield sleeps while rooks hover in the distance, so black against the white world, the trees alive with their endless, idle chatter.

ALMOST overnight, warm southerly breezes melt the last white traces of winter and restore Rockfield to its true spring colours. Soft white clouds steal across the sky, but move too fast to put the hills in shade for long.

Young Rook, now mature, takes a mate for the first time. The old oak tree, home to countless generations of rooks, is occupied once more, its branches the scaffolding for breeding birds to make repairs to last year's nests. Throughout the winter, the impatient birds visited the tree daily and made several attempts to nest during February and early March, but nature played one of her wicked tricks and delayed the breeding season.

At last, the tree is in leaf and the crowded colony loud with deep, hoarse cawing – a chaos of mischievous characters caught in continual argument. But behind this apparent confusion lies a strong sense of order and a stubborn determination to defend territorial rights. Loyalty to his neighbour, and more important, loyalty to his mate for life, is the first lesson Rook will learn on joining the rookery. Aware of his new responsibilities, he flies to the wood to collect twigs for his nest.

SPRING arrives in Rockfield at last. The sun casts long thin shadows through the silver birches while two magpies in flight promise joy to all who see them pass. Black-faced and white-faced lambs are scattered across the rich, green hills and upstream the herons are nesting – living like the rooks in large colonies. The farmer works in the rough, ploughed fields sowing crops and planting vegetables.

The land bursts with new life and against a splendid background of bluebells and daffodils, the courtship ritual begins. With appropriate drama and perfect confidence, Rook performs before his chosen mate. He fans his tail and bows and offers her earthworms as a token of his friendship. Timidly, she responds, begging attention like a juvenile. And as the sun begins to fade and lose its heat, they fly together to the oak tree, the riotous music of the rookery echoing throughout the entire valley of Deepholm.

APRIL gives way to May but leaves behind her winds and stormy showers. To compensate, she paints a rainbow to cast its peaceful colours across Rook's playground. The rain soon passes and the wet grass glistens in the bright sunlight.

Rook pauses by the nest, a proud but weary parent. He flies many miles each day to collect worms and leatherjackets. When these are in short supply, he raids the vegetable crops for potatoes and turnips, and steals newly sown grain from the fields. He can never carry enough to satisfy his whole family and must make apparently endless flights. Despite his efforts, a fledgling, smaller and weaker than the other two, dies. Rook has fought bravely to protect them all from rogues and robbers cast out from other rookeries, while his mate has remained faithfully at the nest. She will not leave until her young can fend for themselves. In four weeks they will be ready to fly with the flock.

IT IS JUNE and the young rooks are flying. Scarcely have they learned the joys of flight when they fall victim to the farmer's gun. Blind to their innocence, he shoots them down while the other rooks fly round in panic and distress, unable to rest until the thunderous sound is silenced by the night.

Morning breaks. A scattering of black feathers blown carelessly around by the breeze serve as the only reminder of yesterday's slaughter. The dead birds have been snatched up overnight by hungry foxes. Rook has paid a high price for living off land controlled by man and has lost another fledgling. Rooks dig in the stubble for beetles, weevils and wireworms. A sentry watches from a nearby tree for the man with the gun. But he is at work on the harvest and will not come again until next spring. Then he will again misjudge the rook, failing to recognise this bird as his ally against the pests which ruin his crops.

Rook introduces his son to the flock to establish his position in the pecking order, a rigid hierarchy controlled by the wiser, more arrogant rooks who feed first and no doubt live longest. Soon Rook's son will form his own flock and follow his own chosen code of behaviour.

It is a warm day late in July. There is little wind to shift the clouds and the sun hides away for hours behind the haze. The young rooks form new flocks and explore distant places but many of them still return to the old familiar rookery at nightfall.

Food is now difficult to find, as from June the earthworms decrease in number. Rook leads his son to the oak woods to collect caterpillars and to the meadows to catch the insects swarming round the poppies. A kestrel hovers close by. For a moment, Rook is alert, but there is no danger to his offspring. Only a buzzard or a red kite could threaten his life now he is fully grown. But for at least another year he will be without the glossy blue feathers and white patch at the base of the beak, the markings of a fully mature bird.

A heron glides by, the gentle giant of the sky. His large wings cast mysterious shadows as he passes – like a relic of a distant time. His favourite tree, the elm, stands diseased and leafless, its branches too brittle to bear the weight of breeding herons, and long since abandoned by rooks who are always first to sense the smell of death. Sadly, like tall, grey pencil skeletons, the elm trees fade away – scattered across a landscape, which, for now, is still green and growing.

AUGUST passes to make way for September with its clear nights and crisp cold mornings. The midday sun sits low in the sky and in the late afternoon the shadows stretch far into the distance. Rooks fly across a backcloth of rich, autumn golds, the trees still holding their leaves, but now fast on the turn, greens fading into yellows with the approach of the new season.

The horse chestnut covers the ground with conkers and the gorse comes into flower. Blackberries ripen in the hedgerows and rooks feed on fallen apples in the orchards, while the farmer, at a safe distance, ploughs the fields and prepares seed-beds for oats and barley.

The rooks are unsettled and are starting to leave their rookeries to nest in Brooksholm Wood for the winter. At this time, they are joined by other migrating rooks from northern Europe. With many new young birds in the flock, the older rooks periodically hold parliaments to administer justice, to kill off the sick, and to punish thieves, traitors and lawbreakers. As many as a hundred birds may take part in this strange ritual.

Strong shafts of sunlight emerge from the cloud bank and filter across the beechwood floor, giving the fallen leaves and bracken a fireside glow. Suddenly, the rooks gather in a large circle and close in on an unfortunate bird. They attack from every side. After a great deal of noise and fierce argument, the crowd disbands, leaving their victim to his fate. This one is lucky, he can fly and has suffered damage only to his tail feathers. We shall never know his crime, but can be sure he will not return to Rockfield to make the same mistake again.

IN THIS mild October of mist and rain and little wind, some trees still hold their autumn colours. The swallows and other summer visitors are now fast on the move and huge flocks of European starlings wheel noisily around their pine tree roosts.

Toadstools burst from the soil, now thick with damp, decaying leaves and the countryside is draped with gossamer – the cobwebs of young spiders who travel great distances across their delicate silvery lacework.

The rooks relish the seasonal feast of fruit and nuts and fatten themselves up in readiness for the long winter ahead. Squirrels briskly collect seeds, fungi and fallen acorns and store them in secret places. The rooks have also taken to hoarding and burying and take acorns from the tree, carrying as many as three or four in their pouches each time. They break the hard shells by smashing them against stones.

Thick mists drift across the fields and Rook and his family hurriedly bury their treasure. In the distance, the rooks of Rockfield take to the skies and perform their aerial wizardry, as if to celebrate the autumn harvest. They climb into the sky, then make sudden, rapid dives towards the trees, but appear to regain control just in time to climb again and complete yet another circuit. They glide effortlessly on the air currents and are too high now for the human eye to follow, drifting out of sight, in search of new horizons.

Novemer brings the cold North winds, the hail and rain, and winter comes again to Rockfield. All the leaves have fallen to reveal the delicate framework of bare trees. The air is still, the sky without cloud. Overnight, the temperature falls to freezing.

The first light of morning unveils a fairyland. Each twig and blade of grass is outlined with frozen dew and the hills are distanced by a blue haze. The nearby trees and hedges are clean and crisp and the whole world glistens with a magic silvering of hoar frost.

The rooks wake early and circle the wood briefly before flying to the fields. Feeding will be difficult until the sun breaks through the mist and melts the frozen surface.

Rook sits on Little Ancre Hill and gazes beyond Deepholm, possibly for the last time. His mate waits nervously by his side while somewhere across the fields, their young offspring flies freely with the flock. Rook knows the time has come to explore new territory and visit other rookeries. Some birds will travel as many as three hundred miles before returning in the spring. But some will not return at all. Rook needs to experience new dangers and attain the wisdom of older birds who have travelled far and wide during their twenty years. With new determination he flies off towards Pyefinch Wood. His mate follows; together they cast their fate to the wind, travelling the way of the crow, following an uncertain route over land and sea.

IN DECEMBER, as the sun goes down and Rockfield sleeps, rooks and jackdaws can be seen journeying home to their roosts, trailing for miles in long, broken threads across the skyline. They have been feeding on the stubble, the ground still soft and moist and alive with insects.

Despite the uncertain start, this year has been kind to rooks. The summer has not been too dry, the autumn rich in acorns and the winter, as yet, has brought little snow. As the farmer knows, when rooks nest high in the trees, the summer will be good. But if they desert their rookeries altogether it is a bad omen and a sign of disaster to come. Fortunately this is rare and rooks usually return to the same trees year after year.

With January and the worst of the winter weather on its way, rooks will soon have to face continual overnight frosts, ice and deep snowdrifts. But for now they are undaunted and are in excellent spirits, visiting Rockfield village at dusk to swoop and dive among the chimney pots. They float drunkenly through the smoke, enjoying the heat, to rise like the Phoenix from the fumes.

And as the last traces of golden light vanish behind the trees and the haunting moon rises, rooks circle and settle at last into the shadows of the night, to rest peacefully until the dawn.

First published in Great Britain 1980 by
Hamish Hamilton Children's Books
Garden House, 57-59 Long Acre, London WC2E 9JZ

The author gratefully acknowledges the assistance of Malcolm Smythe in the design and layout of this book.

British Library Cataloguing in Publication Data
King, Deborah
1. Rook

2. Birds – Wales – Rockfield region
I. Title
598.8'64   QL696.P2367
ISBN 0 241 10372 X

Printed in Great Britain by
Fakenham Press Limited,
Fakenham, Norfolk. .

*In the sale of original paintings
the artist is represented by
Portal Gallery Ltd
London*